COLLAGE and
CONSTRUCTION

OTHER TITLES BY THE SAME AUTHOR IN THE
BEGINNING ARTIST'S LIBRARY

1. SCULPTURE: *Clay, Wood & Wire*   4. CRAFTS: *Sticks, Spools & Feathers*

2. PRINTMAKING: *Paper, Ink & Roller*   5. CERAMICS: *Ceramics—From Clay to Kiln*

3. DRAWING: *Pencil, Pen & Brush*   6. PAINTING: *Paint, Brush & Palette*

7. PHOTOGRAPHY: *Lens and Shutter*

Copyright © 1970 by Harvey Weiss. All Rights Reserved
Young Scott Books. A Division of Addison-Wesley Publishing Company, Inc., Reading, Massachusetts 01867
Library of Congress Catalog Card Number 76–98115 ISBN: 0–201–09163–1
Printed in the United States of America

COLLAGE and CONSTRUCTION

by Harvey Weiss

YOUNG SCOTT BOOKS

Table of Contents

Introduction   page 7

Getting Started   11

Searching for Material   14

Flags and Banners   19

A Texture Collage   24

Collage as Decoration   28

Paper Constructions   33

Boxes   38

Using Light with Collage
     and Construction   44

Constructions   49

Lines in Space   56

Conclusion   62

The majority of the constructions and collages reproduced in this book were made by the author to illustrate specific ideas and methods of working. Where work in museum collections has been reproduced, the name of the artist and the museum are given in the caption. Other work, not by the author, nor in public collections are: page 15 (upper illustration), student work; page 16 (on the left), student work; page 22 (upper illustration), Elizabeth Weiss; page 22 (bottom), Margaret Morris; page 49, John Weiss; page 54, Margaret Morris; page 58 (bottom), John Weiss; page 59 (upper left), Faith Kiermaier. The reed construction shown on page 63 was assembled by a group of sculptors and suspended by helium-filled weather balloons over a park in New York City to celebrate the opening of an outdoor sculpture exhibition by the Sculptors Guild.

The author wishes to thank the following organizations and individuals who have been generous in their help and assistance in the preparation of this book: the Museum of Modern Art, New York; the Museum of Modern Art, Stockholm, Sweden; the Philadelphia Museum of Art; the Pasadena Art Museum; the Bertha Schaefer Gallery; Kunio Izuka; and Margaret Morris, teachers staff, Institute of Modern Art.

MERZ *(With the Letters "Elikan" Repeated), Kurt Schwitters. Museum of Modern Art, New York. This collage uses cut paper, candy wrappers, advertisements.*

Introduction

Some Definitions

When a number of different materials are pasted together to create a work of art we have what is called a *collage*. The word comes from the French word meaning "to paste." It is pronounced *coal-ahzh*.

When the materials assembled are more solid, and the work turns out to be three-dimensional it is called a *construction*. As the name implies, you build up, or construct something. The illustration on the left above is a collage. The other is a construction.

Why?

Collage and construction have fascinated a great many artists because they are very different from the usual art techniques. An ordinary painting or sculpture starts with a clean palette and fresh paints — or a block of wood or tub of clay.

When you set about making a collage or construction you start with a collection of miscellaneous "junk"— bits and pieces and castoffs and clippings and whatnots. And these varied odds and ends will usually suggest to you what to do. In other words, you aren't likely to come to your materials with a clear idea of what you are going to make. Rather, you come to your materials with an open mind — and let your materials *tell you* what to make. This is quite a turnabout from the usual art approach and is one of the things that makes this way of working so very interesting.

This construction makes use of a cork ball, two feathers, a paper cup, a roll of tape, three sticks, an old electric meter, a cardboard tube, and a swatch of rug.

The Open Eye

As you can see, the kinds of materials you gather will have a lot to do with the sort of results you get. The collage artist doesn't usually go out looking for specific things. He is more likely to clip photographs and pictures he finds interesting, or he will wander about picking and choosing odds and ends — bits of wood or metal, scraps of cloth, twigs, paper, pebbles — out of the rubble and junk that can be found everywhere.

It might at first appear that little effort is needed to gather a lot of miscellaneous material. And yet it does require thought and judgment, because you can't collect *everything* you see. You must select what has a particular quality, or interest, or what is suggestive and will in some way lend itself to a collage or construction.

The Putting Together of...

Of course it is not enough simply to gather objects you find interesting and suggestive. A pile of odds and ends, no matter how interesting individually, is not much to look at. The materials you decide to use must be *arranged* and *combined* to make a dramatic, pleasing composition.

The Most Important Ingredient

The one thing you must have when you make collages and constructions is imagination! You must be willing to try different combinations of materials and objects. You must experiment with shapes and colors and images and ideas. With collage this is not hard to do. You can arrange and rearrange the elements you have chosen before they are finally and permanently fastened down. You can shift, cut, modify, add, or eliminate and change your mind — and then change it again — until you finally get something you are satisfied with.

Collage and construction are for those who are willing to give anything a try — for those who think even the wildest and most unlikely idea is worth investigating. It is a way of working for the adventurous, the carefree, and the brave!

MAQUETTE FOR NUIT DE NOEL, *Henri Matisse.*
Museum of Modern Art, New York.
This collage is actually a preliminary study
for a large stained-glass window.

Getting Started

This chapter will show you some of the different ways of making a collage with materials that everybody can find around the house. They consist simply of a newspaper or magazine and the odds and ends that can be found in any family sewing box.

Using the illustrations on this and the next two pages as a guide and reference, you can make a variety of collages yourself. Remember though, that the illustrations suggest only a few of the possibilities and ways of working. They are intended to get you started making collages on your own.

First gather your materials. Get thread, ribbons, buttons, spools, yarn, pins, and any scraps of fabric or lace or fur or whatever else of this sort you can find. You'll also need a newspaper or magazine and a good-sized table on which to work.

THE TOOLS: For paper collage the most important tool is a pair of good, sharp scissors. For very delicate cutting, a single-edged razor is also useful. Don't ever be tempted to use a double-edged razor. This is an extremely dangerous item.

A white casein glue such as Elmer's is excellent for pasting. It should be applied with a large, soft brush, rather than squeezed out and used in little droplets. If the glue you are using seems too thick, add water. Wallpaper paste and library paste are also suitable. Wallpaper paste is particularly good for pasting down large pieces of paper. It is slow-drying and lets you smooth out your paper so that there are no wrinkles or unglued edges. Rubber cement should be used only as a last resort, because it is rather messy, impermanent, and likely to stain. When heavier and more awkward objects must be fastened on a collage, model-making cement or a casein glue is best. These are fairly thick, they dry fast, and are extremely strong.

You will also need a supply of good, stiff cardboard to use as a base to which you can attach your materials. This is particularly important if you are going to use heavy materials. Otherwise, you could get by with a simple large sheet of paper for a background.

You will find that if you glue more than one or two small pictures onto a cardboard background, it will begin to warp. You can counteract this by gluing a large piece of paper to the *underside* of the cardboard.

The collages illustrated on these pages have been made from the materials already mentioned. One is realistic, one is a design, and another two are concerned with mood and idea. These three different approaches should suggest to you ways of making your own collages.

1. The collage shown on page 10 is *realistic*. Buttons make the eyes. The mouth is a piece of wool yarn. The head is a lace doily. This collage is not very accurate, nor a specific portrait, but it does depict someone or something that actually exists. Try making an animal, a car, or a house out of the yarn, buttons, pins, and other odds and ends you have collected.

2. The collage above is a *design*. It isn't a picture of anyone or anything. It doesn't tell a story. It is an arrangement of shapes, patterns, and colors which simply look well together.

3. The two collages shown on the opposite page are quite a different matter. Neither is very much concerned with looking pleasant or pretty. The collage on the left is rather horrible

and shocking. The idea of a little baby playing with a large rattlesnake is a frightening idea. The photograph of the baby and the one of the snake were cut out and placed together solely for the purpose of making an unexpected and surprising image. The little black beads, which came from the sewing box, add another sinister element to the collage.

One of the most interesting things about collage is its ability to take common, ordinary pictures and combine them with other common, ordinary pictures to produce an entirely new and *uncommon* image. This is what has occurred with the baby and the snake.

Many artists today—and especially those who make collages and constructions—are not concerned with creating "pretty" pictures. They are more interested in making pictures or objects which will surprise, excite, shock, inform—sometimes even puzzle or disgust the viewer. They want him to react to their work, not just idly glance at it. They want to involve the viewer in their art.

In the collage above right, the materials from the sewing box have been used to express the idea of combat, or war. This too, is a not-very-pretty collage. The needles and pins and razor blades are threatening and dangerous. On the left, the opposing forces are dark and evil, and that bee is certainly up to no good!

Try making a collage that suggests some of the problems that concern you — air or water pollution, the dangers of smoking, the ugliness of littering, for example.

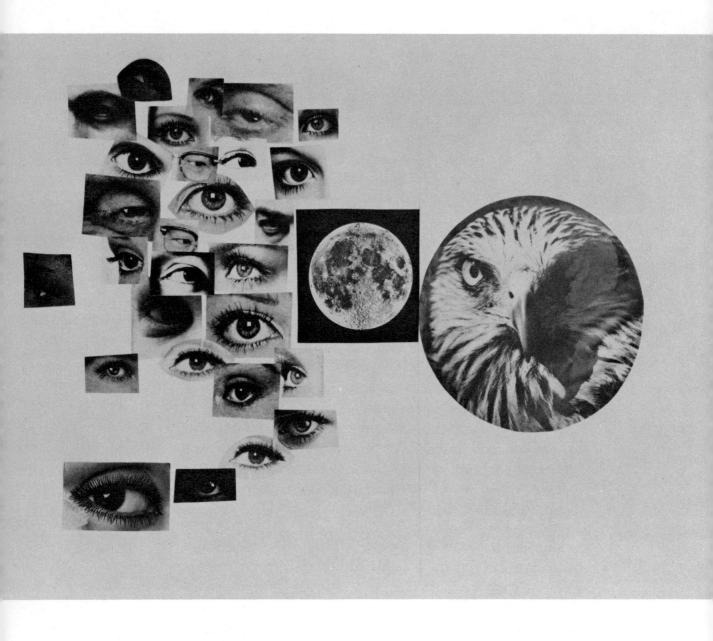

Searching for Material

One of the most important aspects of collage and construction making is collecting material. The more material you gather and the greater its variety, the better the chances are of your work turning out well.

What sort of things should you look for? Anything and everything! It is better to have too much to choose from than not enough.

Collect old magazines and all sorts of printed material. Go through magazines, ripping out pages that have a lot of color and pattern and interesting people and objects. Try not to be distracted simply by prettiness. If you come across a picture of a beautiful tree there is no point in cutting it out just because it is beautiful. However, if you think that the colors or patterns of the leaves, or the texture of the bark is interesting, or if you think the tree might be useful in combination with something else, then cut it out and save it for possible use in the future.

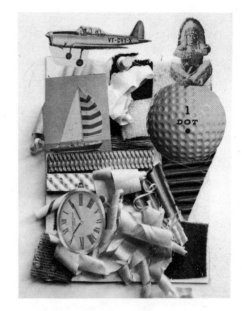

The collage below was made from advertising headlines clipped out of one issue of a magazine. The large letters—both black on white, and white on black—were cut apart and re-arranged with an eye to their patterns and shapes rather than their message.

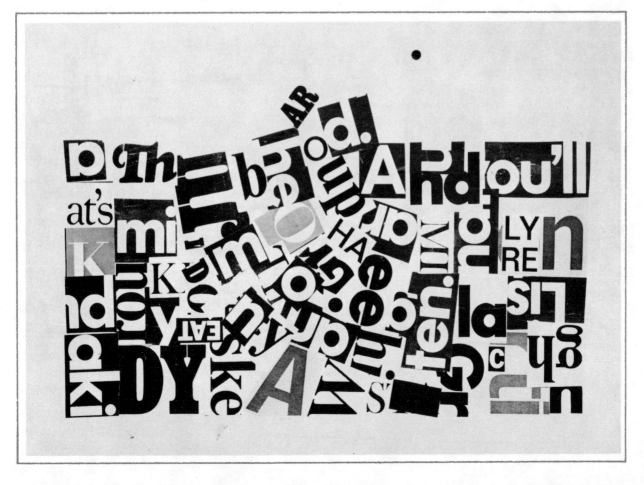

If you poke about in the backs of closets, or in old bureau drawers, you are likely to find all sorts of usable materials. Somewhere in your house or apartment there is bound to be an old rag drawer, and in it you should be able to find bits of lace or patterned fabrics that can be put to good use. The collage on the left is made of a few odd cloth scraps and some black paper. Most households also have at least one box full of miscellaneous junk—broken tools, bottle caps, bits of metal, wire, wood, screws, and so on.

If you live in the country, or have an opportunity to walk through fields and woods you'll find many natural materials that can be used, such as leaves, pebbles, dried grasses, bark, etc. The collage below right, is made from twigs. They were carefully arranged on a plywood background, and held in place with a white casein glue.

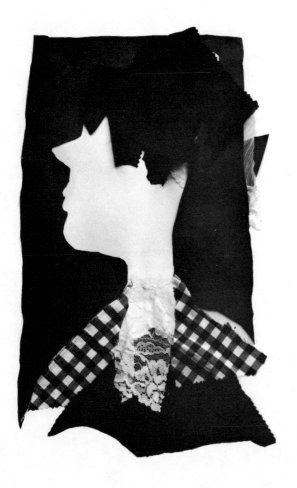
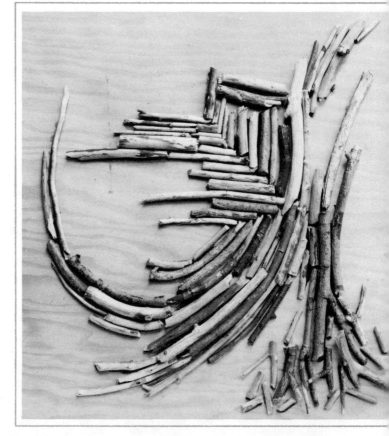

SKY CATHEDRAL, *Louise Nelson. Museum of Modern Art, New York. This construction, by one of America's best known artists, is over eleven feet tall. It is built entirely of odd scraps of wood—boxes, old chair legs, pieces of wooden banisters, weathered boards, and scraps of molding and driftwood. The entire construction is painted a flat black.*

An empty lot or your town dump will always have litter and discarded junk that can be used in a collage or construction. It has been said that the artist who makes collages and constructions is first cousin to a ragpicker and junk man. As already discussed in the introduction, you must keep an open eye, but at the same time use your judgment as you walk about collecting materials. You are not going to get a very friendly reception at home if you walk in with a leaking carton of evil-smelling rubbish that will collapse in the middle of the living-room floor.

Although we have discussed at length the sort of old, discarded, used materials usually used for collage and construction, it is also possible and quite common to work with new materials such as cardboard, paper of various sorts, new wood, plastic, and so on. (And there is no reason why both new and old materials cannot be combined.) Some of the constructions discussed later in the book make very considerable use of fresh, new materials.

MERZ CONSTRUCTION, *Kurt Schwitters. Philadelphia Museum of Art. Sometimes it is difficult to tell the difference between a collage and a construction. This piece is called a construction because some of the materials used are quite massive and project outward a considerable distance.*

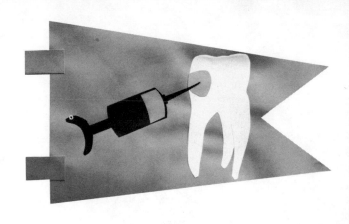

Flags and Banners

Do you have your own flag? Everybody should have one. In medieval times, any knight worth his salt carried a flag bearing his own personal design. It is a fashion that has somehow gone out of style. But there is no reason why you shouldn't design and make your own flag or banner. You can snip and cut and adjust and change and experiment until you get a design that just suits you.

Some flag and banner designs are based on the initials of the owner, others on a symbol of the field in which he is interested. For example, what could be more appropriate for a dentist than the flag shown on the right, above! The one below it is based on the initial A.

Banners like those shown here are a simple form of collage using colored and patterned papers pasted together. Do you prefer very bright colors or soft, harmonious colors? You will find that your banner will look better if you limit the number of colors you use. Too many strong colors are confusing and will not look as bright from a distance. Keep in mind that a simple, uncluttered style is also better when you are cutting out and choosing shapes. Many complicated, small shapes will look cluttered and lost.

As you work on your banner, lay out all the different parts before you do any pasting. You can shift about and modify the design until it looks just right to you. Then it can be permanently fastened together.

When making flags or banners—or for that matter collages, constructions, or any art—don't settle for the first, obvious idea that comes to mind.

For example, when most people think of "flag," what comes to mind is a rectangular shape like the shape of most national flags, or perhaps a triangular pennant. But why not create an

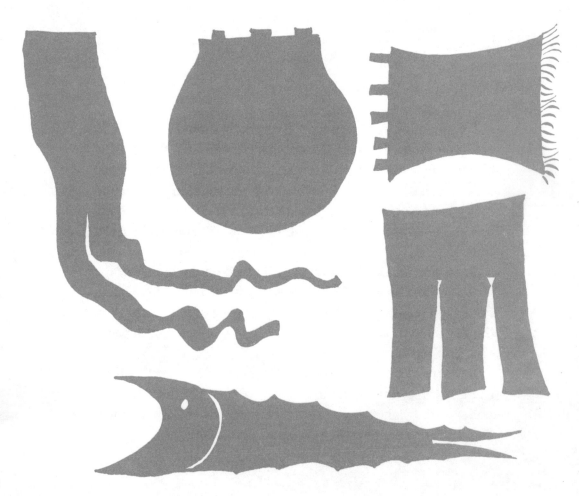

unconventional shape or use materials other than paper or fabric?

If you *do* happen to have a flagpole in your front yard and want to fly a flag from it, you can't be as completely free as you might like. It must be rugged enough to flap in a strong wind without falling apart.

The "octopus flag" shown here manages to be unconventional in shape, but nevertheless quite functional. The "tentacles" flap about in a very lively fashion in even a slight breeze. The upper part of this flag contains a large, partially inflated balloon between the two layers of felt. This gives the octopus a little thickness on top. A stiff brass wire is sewn along the upper edge to help the flag maintain its shape.

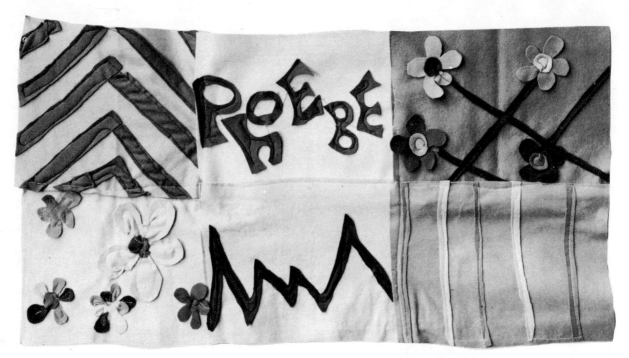

This flag was made for use on a boat (whose name is the Phoebe.) *It is made of felt.*

Using Fabrics

Banners and flags can be made with fabrics rather than paper and of course, will be much more permanent. But now you'll probably have to do a great deal of sewing instead of pasting. (If you have all the parts of your banner cut to size and pinned in place you may be able to pursuade someone with a sewing machine to stitch it all together for you.)

If you're not too fussy you can use other means of attaching things to your banner. A casein glue can be used, as well as staples, pins, or even nuts and bolts!

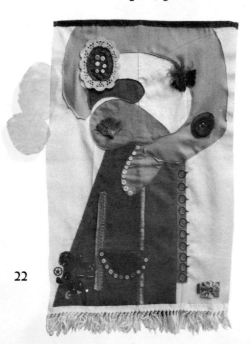

The banner on the left uses a great variety of materials. The basic, rectangular shape is white felt. But cotton prints, velvet, satin, and various other fabrics are used as well as buttons, satin bows, brass loops and a fringe along the bottom. In the lower left corner you may be able to see the insides of an old alarm clock. Some of these materials have been sewed on, others attached with glue.

CHASUBLE, *Henri Matisse. Museum of Modern Art, New York. A chasuble is a wide sleeveless cloak worn by priests. This one is made of satin, silk, and velvet.*

Your biggest problem with a cloth banner will be to locate suitable fabrics in colors you like. Felt comes in many colors and is ideal for flags and banners because it is quite strong and doesn't unravel.

There are several different ways to hang your completed banner which are nicer than just thumbtacking it to your wall. The drawings below show how you can use wooden dowels to good advantage.

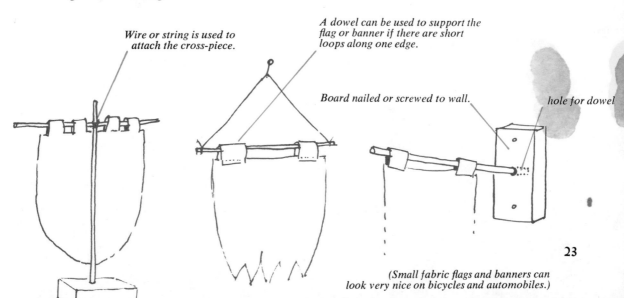

Wire or string is used to attach the cross-piece.

A dowel can be used to support the flag or banner if there are short loops along one edge.

Board nailed or screwed to wall.

hole for dowel

(Small fabric flags and banners can look very nice on bicycles and automobiles.)

23

A Texture Collage

Texture is the *feel* of a surface. Satin has a smooth texture; sandpaper a rough texture. Texture is an additional element that will enrich and enliven a collage. It adds variety and interest.

The textures you use in a collage may be either real or illusory. For example, you could cut out a photograph of a piece of bark and use that in your collage. Or you could get the actual piece of bark, and use that. The photograph is illusory—the bark itself is the real thing. These two different kinds of textures are often used by collage makers.

As you can see from the opposite page, almost anything that will stick with glue or paste can be included in a collage. Try making a small collage yourself, using only varied textures, to see what results you can get. If you use a strongly contrasting selection of textures imaginatively, you will have an interesting collage.

The three collages on the opposite page were made to demonstrate how textures can be used. The top collage shows what a great variety you can have. This panel has everything from the smoothest glass to a rough rasp, from soft sponge rubber to sharp aluminum opening tabs from soft drink cans.

The center collage was made in a somewhat different way. A fairly thick layer of glue was spread over the background. Then different textures were produced by sprinkling a variety of smaller, more delicate materials onto the wet glue. Sawdust, dried grass, sand, tea leaves, matches were some of the materials used.

The bottom illustration is a "soft" collage. The materials used are soft—rubber, velvet, a frayed end of nylon rope, a bit of carpeting, a piece of fur.

In each of these collages the main interest has been in the variety of textures. There have been no carefully designed color schemes or thoughtfully planned compositions. It is just the simple pleasure of varied textures, neatly fastened together, that make these collages fun to make, to touch, and to look at.

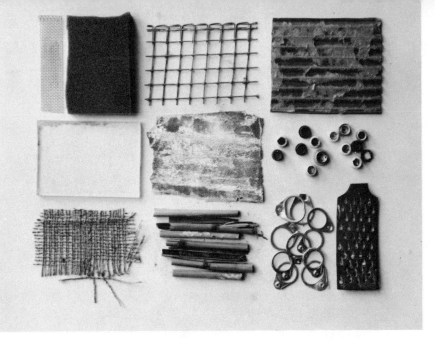

The collage above was made in order to demonstrate how a texture can be created by using small, white beans. The center area has a jumbled pattern which is surrounded by an even and orderly pattern.

The collage below uses dark kidney beans as well as the plain white beans. In this case the colors and textures of the beans have been placed to create a carefully worked-out arrangement of shapes. If you rummage around in your kitchen you're more than likely going to find a variety of foods — split peas, coffee beans, macaroni, etc., that lend themselves to this kind of collage.

If you want to try making a collage of this sort, gather your materials, then spread a thick layer of glue on your background, a small section at a time. Then put your materials in place. This way is simpler and faster than putting a dab of glue on each individual bean.

The collage below uses much heavier, more solid materials. Driftwood, weatherworn scraps of wood, spools were collected and fastened by means of nails and glue to a plywood background. In one place the nails themselves are used as texture. (If a collage like this were constructed so that it could stand up by itself, without the background, it would be called a construction.)

Collage as Decoration

The technique of collage can be put to many practical uses. It can be used to decorate a great variety of objects. A few possibilities are shown on these pages. The pencil holder is made from a can which is covered with a strip of paper upon which a cut-out design is pasted. A small jar with straight sides will also do for this. Part of a heavy cardboard mailing tube has been used to make the "musical notes" pencil holder.

Wastepaper baskets are often pretty dreary-looking objects. But they can be made more attractive if covered with a bright and lively collage design. Simple, paper lampshades can also be covered in a similar manner.

The lampshade on the opposite page uses plain, wedge-shaped strips cut from magazines. However, the clippings have been chosen with great care and thought so as to get interesting combinations of colors, textures, and subjects. When you use clippings of this sort on a lampshade you must be aware of what is printed on the *reverse* side because it will show through when the lamp is turned on. This can complicate your selections.

Various kinds of small boxes are also quite suitable for decoration. You may be able to find some cigar boxes or tin file boxes which you can cover. You can make them to hold jewelry, file cards, sewing materials, and all sorts of things.

When you set about to cover a box or container of some sort try to find a theme or idea before you start. Don't just paste on a miscellaneous batch of pretty pictures. That's likely to be rather boring.

When you glue down your paper be particularly careful to use enough glue and to smooth out all air bubbles. The entire area of the paper you are gluing must be firmly attached to its background. There should be no loose edges or dry spots, or your collage will peel or wrinkle.

When a collage is used to cover practical objects which will be put to everyday use, you should cover the surface of the collage with a protective coating of some kind. A thinned-out coating of casein glue works fine. It is possible to use shellac or varnish on some materials; however, they tend to darken many papers such as newspaper. It is advisable to make a test on the

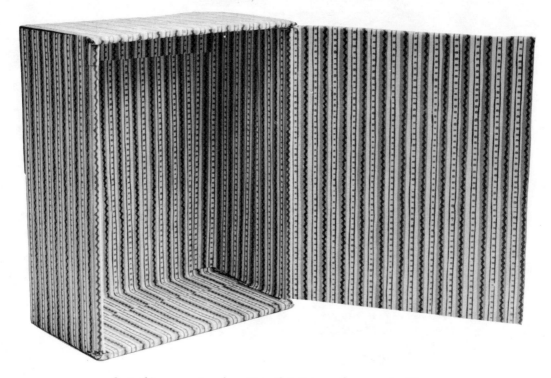

Once this was a cigar box. Now that it is neatly covered with some leftover wallpaper it becomes quite elegant and suitable for storing all sorts of small or delicate objects.

bottom or a back corner before covering your entire, finished work with any shellac or varnish.

The boxes shown here are examples of how a basic theme is used. The theme of the jewel box on the right, above, is rather obviously "jewelry." The box below it is actually a savings bank. The entire box is covered with newspaper accounts of financial dealings. The drawing in the margin shows how this box is constructed. The top piece is not nailed down. It is held in place only by the glued paper. To get the money out you must cut through the paper so that the top will come off.

The box at the bottom of the page is covered with feathers —inside and outside! It doesn't serve any practical purpose at all. It contains an egg onto which sequins are pasted. (The inside of the egg was removed by punching a small hole in top and bottom and then blowing out the contents.) This box is just plain silly.

Paper Constructions

You might associate paper only with collage since it is not really three-dimensional. But there are kinds of paper which are stiff and strong. And there are ways of rolling or folding paper so that it becomes quite rigid.

You can use paper to make designs that are, on the one hand, engineered structures, and on the other hand, handsome, or even beautiful objects.

The kind of paper you use is important. You won't get good results from old newspapers or facial tissue. Heavy, stiff drawing paper is good. Bristol board, tag board, the kind of heavy board used in cartons and in laundry boxes is excellent. Corrugated board can also be used. Although construction paper is not as strong, it is handy to have because it comes in so many different colors.

Below and on the next page are shown a few basic tricks which will help you with the mechanics of putting a paper construction together, and you'll probably invent a few of your own once you get started.

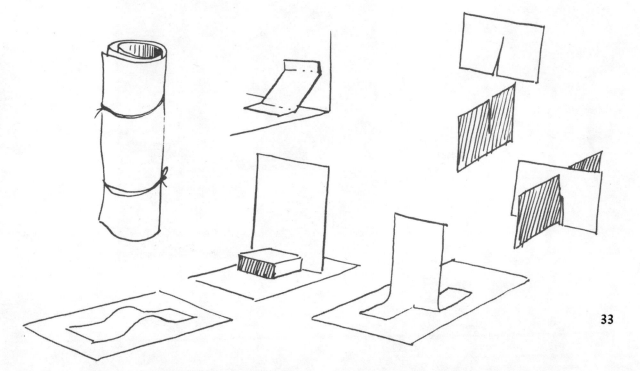

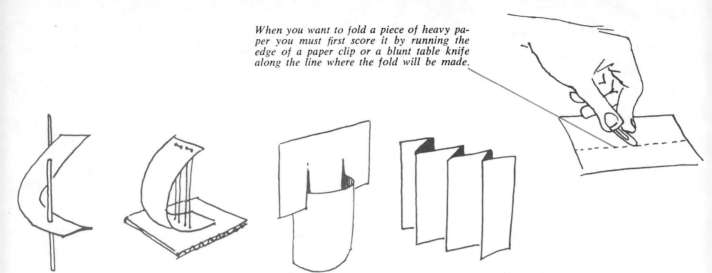

When you want to fold a piece of heavy paper you must first score it by running the edge of a paper clip or a blunt table knife along the line where the fold will be made.

One of the big advantages of paper constructions is that they are very lightweight. This means that you can easily hang a construction from the ceiling where it will look very dramatic. Or you can fasten it on the top of a long rod, as illustrated below, and it will gently sway back and forth whenever a breeze strikes it.

When you build a construction you must remember that you are now making a sculptural object. It will be seen from all sides, not just the front. Keep turning it as you work on it so that you'll see how it looks from all points of view.

34

Wallpaper or cloth can be glued onto cardboard and used as shown here.

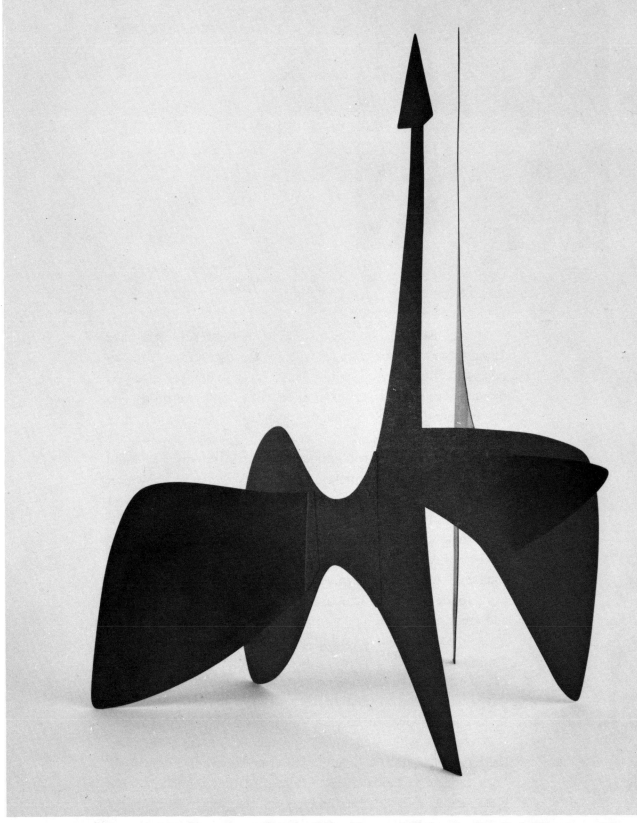

MODEL FOR TEODELAPIO-SPOLETO, *Alexander Calder. Museum of Modern Art, New York. This construction (called a stabile) is actually quite large and cut out of sheet aluminum. But it is the sort of construction you could make out of cardboard or any stiff, heavy paper. The one shown here is painted black, but any clean, strong color would look good.*

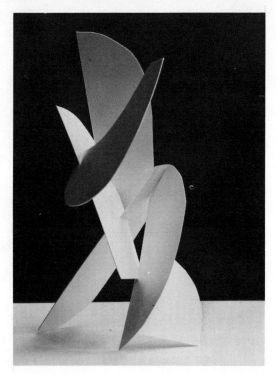

This construction uses stiff, heavy drawing paper. The various parts are notched, so that they fit together. A drop of glue keeps them firmly in place.

Don't hesitate to combine some of the materials you have already used in your collages with your construction. You can add colored paper, clippings, feathers, or whatever else you think will improve the overall effect. But don't overdo it. Too much miscellaneous, added-on decoration can make for a sloppy, cluttered look.

Using paper construction methods it is possible to build quite elaborate model houses, castles, or palaces, as shown on the opposite page. If you are making a structure of any size you may want to glue strips of wood onto the heavy paper or cardboard to strengthen and stiffen some of the walls and roofs.

Use a heavy piece of corrugated board for a base. Small, square blocks of wood will come in handy for attaching the walls to the base and for making corners rigid. If you want to add trees or foliage, you can clip thin twigs from bushes or trees, or twist some wire around a short stick, as shown in the margin. These can be pushed into the corrugated base, and held in place with a drop of glue or cement. If a piece of cardboard warps, remember to glue another piece of paper onto the reverse side. This will straighten it out.

Architects will often make a model house to show their clients what their real house will look like when completed. These are very realistic, accurately constructed models with great detail and quite different from the very fanciful and thoroughly impractical houses shown on the facing page.

UNTITLED (HOTEL DU NORD), *Joseph Cornell.*
Pasadena Art Museum.

CENTRAL PARK CARROUSEL, *Joseph Cornell.*
Museum of Modern Art, New York.

Boxes

When a collage or construction is put together inside a box something special happens. For some reason a theatrical and often mysterious quality results.

The constructions on the top of this page are by Joseph Cornell, an American artist who has been making boxes like this for many years. His boxes are known throughout the world. They are in many important museums, and sell for thousands of dollars. What makes them so special? Most people agree that what distinguishes them is a certain poetic quality. They often seem to be on the verge of disclosing some secret meanings, some odd truth. There are no simple, obvious explanations for the objects contained in these boxes. For example, what is the significance of the ring and the bit of chain and the brass rod? Why is the paint all cracked and peeling? What an odd combination of things—and yet it all seems to fit together in some very correct, mysterious way.

The box shown above and to the right is much more "busy" and cluttered than the others. But it too, in a different way, seems full of unexplained secrets.

It's a simple matter to build a box. Get a length of wood about 1 by 3 inches and about 3 feet long. This will make a box about 8 by 12 inches and 3 inches deep. There is no reason why you can't make a box any other size, of course. You might prefer a very large or small box, or one of different proportions — perhaps more square or more narrow. The back of the box should be fairly sturdy. You can use plywood or composition board or heavy cardboard for this.

If you look around, you may find a ready-made box that will be suitable. You might even use a cigar box if you are willing

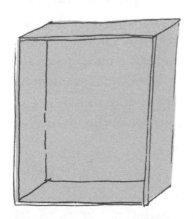
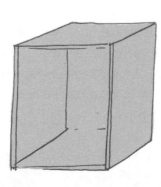

to work on a rather small scale. But do not use any box that is flimsy, wobbly, or too lightweight.

Here are a few hints that may prove helpful: Try to get some major element for the background before you put anything else in the box. This is best done first because a lot of small objects would get in your way if they were already in place. But don't ignore the *sides* of your box. If you are using something large, like a map or a big photograph for a background, it will look very effective if it is pasted up and onto the sides. And you don't have to limit yourself to the interior of your box. There's no reason why your design can't move out, around, and *behind* the box.

Don't hesitate to change your mind or revise your design as you work. Often one element will suggest an entirely new idea, and you might end up with something completely different from what you started out to do.

You will probably find yourself tempted to use strange or unusual materials in your box. Don't worry too much about the logic or reason for what you do. Let your intuition be your guide, and if at some later time you decide to change your mind, you can very easily remove the objects you no longer want and substitute others.

Making *Huntington Bay*

I made the box called *Huntington Bay*, shown on the opposite page. Let me describe to you what I thought about, and how I went about making this box, so that you'll get a firsthand account of how one person works. This may not necessarily be the correct or the best way for you to proceed. But it happens to be the way I worked, and it may give you some ideas.

I started by making the bare wooden box. This is simply a piece of 1-inch by 3-inch board that I cut into two pieces 14 inches long and two pieces 9 inches long. I chose this size for no particular reason other than the proportions seemed pleasant. I nailed the pieces together, making sure the corners were neat and square. Then I traced the outline of this "frame" onto

a piece of Masonite, ⅛ inch thick. I cut the Masonite out and nailed it to the back of the frame. I sanded the edges and corners. Now I had a box.

But what would I do with it? What should I make? My eye happened to glimpse an old marine chart that was tacked to my studio wall. A marine chart is like a road map, except that it shows water depths, coastlines, buoys, and other information of interest to mariners. I decided I would use this chart as a background in the box. I had made a start. Now I felt that the subject for this box would be nautical.

Using wallpaper paste, I glued the chart to the back of the box as well as to all four interior sides. When I finished, the box, as if by magic, had changed character. It was no longer a few scraps of wood. It had taken on a new personality and life of its own. It seemed to me I had created a little self-contained world, or at least a little stage setting which was waiting for the characters and action to begin. This was an exciting moment.

Then I spent a great deal of time simply staring at the box, thinking about what to do next. I finally decided that an old, rough length of rope would contrast well with the soft colors and small, precise details of the chart. And rope is certainly used a great deal on boats. I found a ragged piece of rope in a boatyard nearby and tried placing it in different positions in the box.

It wasn't right. The rope was too dark and seemed rather cute and obvious. I wandered around my studio, poking into dusty corners and behind shelves, and I discovered the old croquet ball with the peeling paint. It didn't have anything in the world to do with the sea or boats, but I liked its color, its texture, and the kind of shadow it made. When I placed the croquet ball in the box, I was very pleased with the way it looked. I drilled a small hole in it and a hole through the back of the box, and fastened it permanently in place with a screw.

Everything in the box was a light color now, and I decided that I liked this effect and should strengthen it. I realized that an additional element without color, such as glass, would help to maintain this light effect. I remembered that I had a large, old magnifying lens somewhere. I finally found it and it looked just fine, adding a little variety to the part of the background chart that was beneath it. At the same time, the glass was a round shape and it repeated the shape of the croquet ball.

Now I had to figure out a way to hold the magnifying glass in place. After a great deal of thought, I decided to file a notch in a short piece of old chair leg. I glued the glass into the notch, and the chair leg to the bottom of the box.

I tried placing two small wooden balls alongside the chair leg and liked the effect they created. I put them there without fastening them down. Then to vary the box, I could shift them around whenever I wished.

I was almost finished now. But I wanted something with a shape that contrasted with all the round shapes. I looked around in boxes of junk and in odd corners and tried a great many different objects. I finally found a twisted piece of wire cable and tried it in the box. It was just right. I drilled a hole in the bottom of the box and inserted the cable. I thought I was finished. But a few days later I happened to be visiting a friend and saw the little toy owl. "I must have it!" I cried, and after much persuasion my friend gave it to me. When I placed it on the top of the wire cable, I knew I was finished at last.

This is the rear of "Huntington Bay." Part of a road map is used to cover the back panel. You can see the head of the screw which holds the croquet ball in place. The short length of rope adds a little variety.

Using Light with Collage and Construction

There is another kind of box similar to those described on the previous pages—but with a built-in source of light. The boxes shown here are like this.

When the light shines on the materials in the boxes, the shadows are strong and sharp, the colors vivid, the highlights intense. Everything becomes theatrical, and you are aware of the action and quality of the light. The light, in fact, becomes one of the elements you have to deal with in the composition.

You can build a box like this exactly the way you built the other boxes, but you must provide a source of light and an opening through which the light can enter the box. The drawings below show several different ways this can be done. If you find

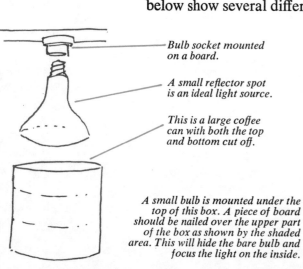

Bulb socket mounted on a board.

A small reflector spot is an ideal light source.

This is a large coffee can with both the top and bottom cut off.

A small bulb is mounted under the top of this box. A piece of board should be nailed over the upper part of the box as shown by the shaded area. This will hide the bare bulb and focus the light on the inside.

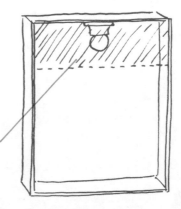

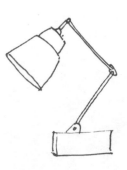

a small, high intensity lamp like the kind shown, you will have the perfect light. If you don't have one of these lamps, you can rig up a bulb and socket in a can, as shown, or even use a flashlight. Since an ordinary flashlight doesn't produce a light that is very strong, you should keep your box in a dark corner where the light, by contrast, would be most effective.

Try to find some very strong textures, strings, mirrors, and various materials that will look especially interesting under light. See if you can find colored, transparent materials such as cellophane, clear plastic, or glass. Glass marbles, a prism, or old lenses will do all sorts of peculiar things when a light shines through them.

In the illustration at the bottom of this page, string has been used to make a very bold design. A great many small holes were drilled around all four sides of the box and two screw eyes were placed at the top and on one side. Then string was threaded back and forth, up and down.

A string construction like this can, of course, be made within any framework (another kind is shown on page 59) but when it is made within a box lighted from above, it is particularly effective.

A well-made light box is not only a handsome thing to look at, but can be very useful as a night light. The bulb is shielded and not very strong, so you can't consider this a lamp to read or work by. However, it can be a practical and pleasant decoration in a dark corner of a room. In the illustration on the right, the bulb and socket are inside the tin can which rests on top of the box.

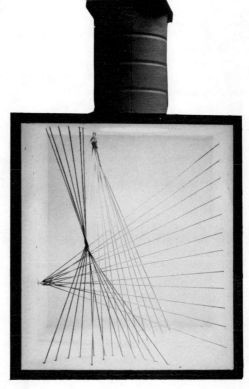

Stained-Glass Windows

You can also use a light box (an empty one) as a background for a collage that uses transparent or translucent materials. This sort of collage will look like a stained-glass window. When light shines through materials like colored glass or cellophane or even thin colored paper, a beautiful jewel-like brilliance is produced. If you've ever seen a stained-glass window in a church or museum you've probably noticed how rich and glowing the colors are.

In both these "windows" the design was first cut out of the large background paper—much the same way you would cut a stencil. Then thin, translucent colored paper was pasted over the back. Plain brown wrapping paper was used as the background for the illustration above. A heavy black paper was used for the "window" on the right.

Several different ways of making paper stained-glass windows are described below. You can attach them to a light box, (which should be painted white inside if it is to be used for this purpose) or tape them to a window and let daylight provide the illumination.

1. Cut shapes out of a piece of heavy, dark paper with a single-edged razor or a sharp stencil knife. Then cover the open spaces with cellophane or the thin tissue paper called "art tissue." This comes in a package of many colors and is available in most art or hobby shops.

2. Stretch a sheet of cellophane or plastic wrap across the front of the light box. Then cut shapes out of colored tissue paper and paste them over this.

3. Still another possibility is to put your materials between two sheets of waxed paper. Then press this "sandwich" with a slightly heated iron. The wax from the paper will melt, sticking the two pieces together and holding the materials firmly in place.

4. It is also possible to cut shapes out of cellophane or tissue paper and join them together with thin strips of tape. A thin black tape is best, but you can also use masking tape. When the "window" is finished and you hold it up to the light, the tape will appear as a thick dark line which divides color areas. This effect is very similar to a real stained-glass window. (Real stained-glass windows, like the one shown below, are made of many separate pieces of colored glass which are joined by means of lead strips. The glass fits into the lead as shown.)

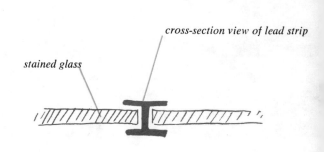

stained glass

cross-section view of lead strip

THE PALACE AT 4 A.M., *Alberto Giacometti. Museum of Modern Art, New York.*

Constructions

The construction shown on this and the next few pages are all composed of a combination of objects. After looking at all the different materials used and the variety of approaches, you might decide that, in constructions, anything goes.

And this is exactly correct. Almost any material, any fanciful notion, or any unlikely combination of found objects can be used. You are limited only by your imagination.

The fact that the artist can work with great freedom, however, does not mean that he uses no judgment. Nor does it mean that he has no idea in his head, or no reason or purpose for what he does. Without an idea or purpose, a construction would be simply a pile of junk.

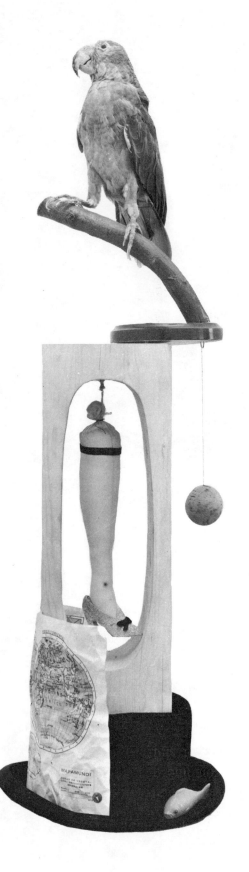

In creating either a collage or a construction, the artist wants to make a design, or suggest a mood or idea, or find a new and uncommon meaning for a group of common objects. The big difference is that construction is a three-dimensional way of working. The materials of construction are more solid and the finished work can be viewed from all sides, like a piece of sculpture.

The construction shown on the left looks good from any point of view. This work consists of a truly strange combination of objects — an old mannequin leg, a map, a plastic fish, a cork ball — and all of this perched on an old derby hat. The effect is mysterious and unreal. It was just this mood that the artist was trying to create.

POETIC OBJECT, *Joan Miró.*
Museum of Modern Art, New York.

The construction above is another matter altogether. This one is concerned with design—with shapes and textures and forms and spaces. It is built carefully like a small piece of furniture with many small parts neatly fitted together. It is actually constructed from long, square-shaped lengths of wood which have been cut into short pieces and glued together. It is a sculptural object.

The construction on page 48 is handled in still another way. The materials here are all light in weight and in feeling. The idea was to make a delicate and birdlike construction, and every object used was chosen with this in mind. The thin sheet of glass, the fragile wood shapes, the thin rods, and open spaces help to suggest this feeling.

Sometimes constructions, like the one by Jean Tinguely on the opposite page, are very elaborate, carefully designed productions. This one contains a number of small electric motors which make everything wiggle and jiggle and at the same time produce various marks and dabs on a slowly unwinding roll of drawing paper.

If you have some small electric motors left over from broken toys or model cars and trains, you may be able to incorporate them into a construction of your own. The motors can make parts of the construction rotate or vibrate or swing back and forth. The small motors which are used in moving advertising displays also lend themselves very nicely to use in constructions.

A walk along a beach produced the materials used in the construction illustrated below. Smooth, white, rounded pebbles were collected along with a handful of flat, dark stones. The thin, white, curved shapes are the sun-bleached jawbones of a small sand shark. The stones were glued directly to the board, along with the lower pair of bones. The upper bones—with the teeth still intact—were fastened to a small wood rod and then fitted into a hole drilled into the board.

METAMATIC, *Jean Tinguely.*
Museum of Modern Art, Stockholm.

Many very dissimilar materials are included in this construction. Objects such as a golf ball, some old chessmen, scraps of wood, a paper cup, parts of an old telephone, and so on, are used. But all these different objects have been given a certain harmony by means of a unifying coat of white paint. Only two or three elements have been left unpainted to provide a contrast.

When you make a construction, just as with a collage, you'll find that very often the materials you've collected will inspire you and get you started. This is how many artists get started. At other times you might have a very definite idea of what you want to do—and *then* hunt around for the materials that will help you execute the idea. For example, you might be at the seashore on a vacation and decide to make a construction about "a day at the beach." In this case, you would probably set out to look for seashells, or driftwood, or sand and beach pebbles, or something to represent the sun (a yellow ball, a light bulb) or an old container of sun lotion, and so on.

There are mechanical problems you will have to solve in any construction. These are largely problems of how to attach one object to another. And the things you combine or attach should stay attached and not fall apart, sag, or shift about when you move or touch them.

There are certain basic materials such as stiff wire, cardboard, wooden dowels, etc. that are very useful when you work on a construction. These will often serve as a framework or armature to which other objects can be attached. The drawings below show a few fastening techniques that may come in handy. But one thing you definitely can't do without is a good deal of ingenuity!

Some Mechanical Tricks

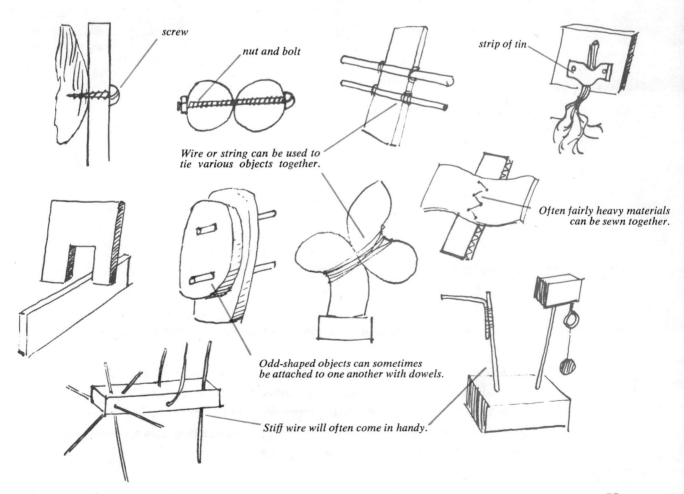

screw

nut and bolt

strip of tin

Wire or string can be used to tie various objects together.

Often fairly heavy materials can be sewn together.

Odd-shaped objects can sometimes be attached to one another with dowels.

Stiff wire will often come in handy.

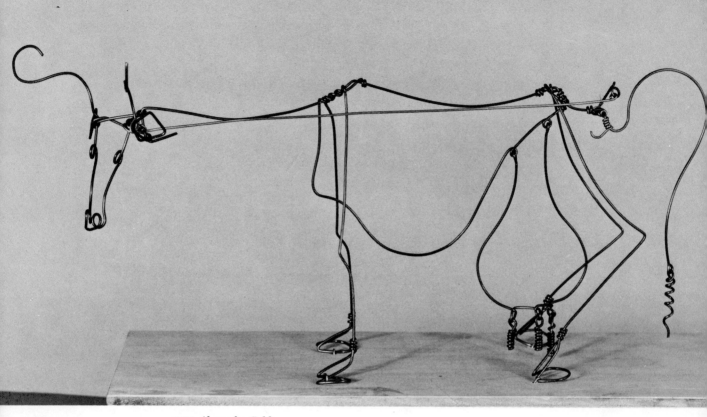

COW, *Alexander Calder.*
Museum of Modern Art, New York.

Lines in Space

A construction doesn't have to be built of solid objects. It
can be built of lines. A construction of this sort is not very different from a pencil or pen-and-ink drawing. In one, you make
a line on a flat piece of paper. In the other, you make a line in
space, using thin rods, or wire, or string, or some other linear
material.

If you are going to make a wire construction you must have
a kind of wire that is suitable. Twenty-two-gauge galvanized
iron wire is good, and any firm copper wire will work well. The
wire you use must be stiff enough so that it won't flop down—
yet soft enough so that you can easily bend it.

A pair of long-nosed pliers is a useful tool for making wire constructions. They will help you bend the wire into small, tight turns and twists. You may also need a wood base unless the construction you make is so designed that it can stand up firmly by itself. "The Cow" by Alexander Calder stands on four legs, so a base to support it is not needed. It is possible to make quite realistic figures or animals using only wire.

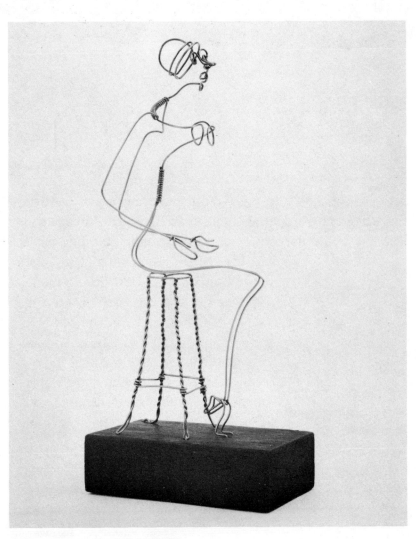

SODA FOUNTAIN, *Alexander Calder.*
Museum of Modern Art, New York.

It is also possible to build quite elaborate linear constructions using many materials other than wire. The construction
illustrated above uses thin wood dowels and stiff white paper.

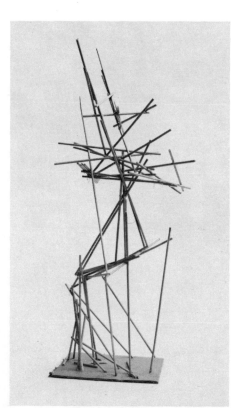

This construction on the left uses
only thin sticks. A fast-drying model-
making cement was used to hold the
sticks together, and a piece of corrugated board served as a base. In making constructions like this and the one
shown above, it is often most conve-
nient to assemble small sections at a
time, letting them lie flat until the
cement dries. Then the various sections
can be glued together and additional
material added as you see fit.

STRING COMPOSITION, *Sue Fuller. Bertha Schaefer*
Gallery. This complex construction is actually built
by stretching many individual strings between two points.

 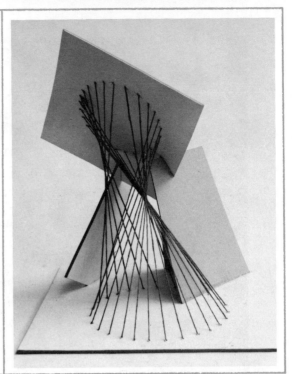

The light box shown on page 45 used a string design within a limited, confined space. Two other ways of using strings are shown on these pages. In the string construction above right, a cardboard structure was built and the string stretched through, around, and over it to make a dramatic design.

The construction illustrated above left uses nails and threads of different colors. The heavy, weathered board which serves as a background (and which is a discarded seat from a swing) makes a strong contrast with the delicate threads and small, shiny nails.

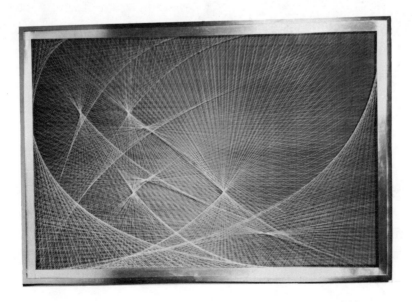

Reeds

The construction in the photograph above is twelve feet high and eight feet across. It is a sprawling, dramatic object, immense in size, very light in weight, and tremendous fun to put together. It is made of reeds.

60

You'll find reeds growing alongside rivers and in low, swampy ground. They sometimes grow as tall as seven or eight feet. They are easily cut with a sharp knife.

If you collect your reeds in spring or early summer, they will be green and flexible. You should spread them out in the sun for a few days to dry out.

The drawing below shows how the reeds are joined. Rubber bands work very well, but if you want to join two reeds at a point other than at their ends you'll have to use something else, such as masking tape, string or thin wire.

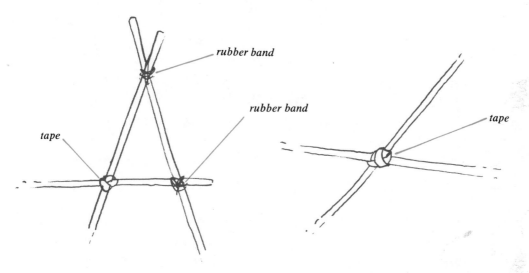

Keep your construction balanced. Too many reeds off to one side will require some kind of counterbalancing weight on the opposite side. As you work, try for an interesting variety of shapes and forms. Bend some of the reeds in order to get curved lines for variety. Contrast congested, busy areas with wide, open areas. Let your construction grow out to the sides as well as straight up. Keep looking at it from all sides. And remember, you want your construction to be a work of art as well as an engineering triumph. (Don't work out-of-doors on a windy day or your construction will think it is a kite!)

If the sort of construction described here appeals to you, but you can't get any reeds, you can do pretty much the same sort of thing on a smaller scale with any thin, light, linear material such as split bamboo, wooden dowels, balsa wood strips, metal rods or even soda straws. A quick-drying cement will be useful with some of these materials as discussed on page 58.

Conclusion

This book has discussed the methods and techniques of collage and construction. It has described some of the different kinds of thinking and some of the different ways of working. But this is only an introduction, a suggestion of the sort of things that you can do. There is such complete freedom and such a variety of possibilities that you must set your own objectives. You can't look to any handbook of instructions, or guidebook, or do-it-by-the-numbers kit to tell you what to do.

What you need is confidence in *your own* ideas, judgments, and imagination. If you decide you would like to try out something, then you must go ahead and try it. If you like what you are making that is reason enough for making it. If you feel your work is not successful—try to figure out where it went wrong— and the next time you'll do better. And if your work does turn out well, that is reason enough to experiment with different materials and new ways of making collages and constructions.

This reed construction was assembled by a group of sculptors and suspended by helium-filled balloons over a park in New York City to celebrate the opening of a sculpture exhibition.

Harvey Weiss, a sculptor as well as a teacher and writer, has exhibitions of his work regularly at the Paul Rosenberg Gallery in New York. Several of his sculptures were recently acquired by the Ford Foundation and presented to various art museums around the United States. His works are in many private collections including those of Joseph H. Hirshhorn and Governor Nelson Rockefeller. He is President of the Sculptors Guild, an organization of professional sculptors.